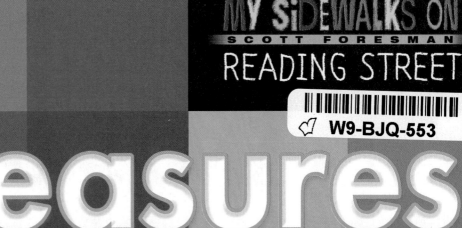

Treasures

Program Authors

Connie Juel, Ph.D.

Jeanne R. Paratore, Ed.D.

Deborah Simmons, Ph.D.

Sharon Vaughn, Ph.D.

Glenview, Illinois
Boston, Massachusetts
Chandler, Arizona
Hoboken, New Jersey

PEARSON

ISBN-13: 978-0-328-45272-9
ISBN-10: 0-328-45272-6

15 16

UNIT 4 Contents

Treasures

Surprising Treasures

Surprise!
How can a surprise be
a treasure?

4

Story Time
How can a story be
a treasure?

34

Treasures in the U.S.A.
What treasures can we
find in the U.S.A.?

64

Treasures to Share

Special Places

Why do we treasure
special places?

86

Treasures at Home

What treasures can we share
at home?

110

Sharing with
Neighbors

What treasures can we
share with neighbors?

136

Contents

Surprise!

Let's Find Out

6 **Surprise!**
Where can you find a surprise?

14 **What Is in the Box?**
See what fits!

22 **The Surprise Party**
Who has a plan for fun?

32 **Riddle Time**
Look for funny clues!

See page 33 for My New Words and Pictionary!

Let's Find Out
Surprise!

Look up at the sky. How big it is! It is big and black.

See the stars. See them shine.
See what the stars make.
Surprise!

Spot the nest in that tree. A chick rests in that nest. That chick will try to fly.

Will the chick fall? Surprise!
It will not. It can fly and fly.

It was wet. Drops made it wet. But now it is dry.

The sun shines in the sky. Can you see red, blue, and green? It is nice. Surprise!

Be still! Ty is home! Ty can spy his pals. He can see their feet.

Some other pals hide by Mom. "Surprise, Ty!" his pals are yelling with smiles. This is fun!

What Is in the Box?

by Fay Marina

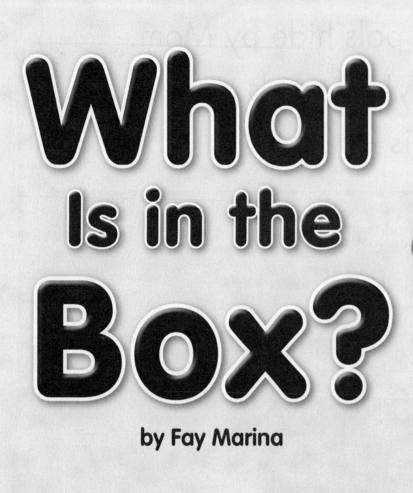

What can go in a box? Look at its size. How big is it? How small is it? Look at its shape. How tall is it? How wide is it?

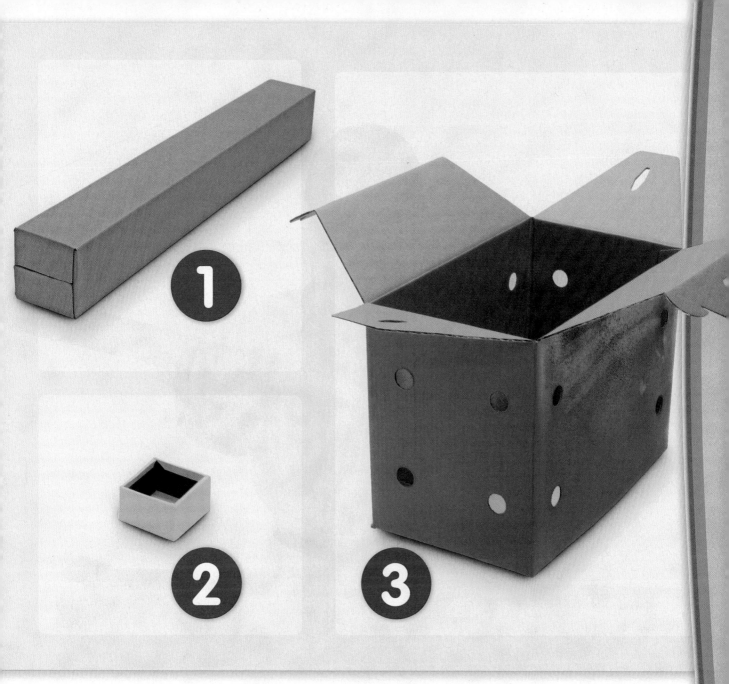

What can go in box 1? What can
go in box 2? What can go in box 3?

This box is skinny. Can a fluffy puppy fit in it? Danny can fit his lucky bat in it. The bat is skinny like this box.

Name some other stuff that can fit in this box. Try!

This box is small. What can fit in a small box? This box has a penny in it. The penny is small like the box.

Try to name some other stuff that can fit in this box.

This box is big. It has holes. It has a big, fluffy bunny and a small, funny bunny in it. They hop, hop in their box.

Try to name some other pets that can go in this box.

The Surprise Party

by Lin Tsang
illustrated by Karen Lee

"It is hot. This path is dusty and bumpy. But the sky is sunny. Trot fast, Trusty, trot fast," said Sir Prize. "I must try to see Queen Wendy."

They rode and rode on that dusty
and bumpy path.

But Sir Prize needed sleep. He made camp by a big lake. The sky had lots and lots of stars.

When the sun came up, Sir Prize
woke up and left his camp.

He rode and rode. Then he saw
some men walking and talking.

"When is their party in that big hall?" one man asked.

"It is at five," the other man said. "We can not be late."

"The party must be for Queen Wendy. It must be a surprise. We, too, can not be late. Trot fast, Trusty, trot fast," said Sir Prize.

"I must stop and get a gift. My, my! How fine this is! I will get this green pin. Queen Wendy will like this fine, green pin," said Sir Prize.

"This is the big hall," Sir Prize said. He peeked in.

Then Queen Wendy and the others yelled, "Surprise, Sir Prize!"

And that did surprise Sir Prize! The party was for him!

Riddle Time

I like to run.

I like to lick.

I would like to fetch a stick.

What am I?

This day comes one time a year.

A happy song is what you hear.

You may get a gift or two.

What happy day is it for you?

Answers: a dog; a birthday

32

My New Words

how*   Tell me **how** to win a prize. **How** long will it take?

other*   Pick one size and not the **other**. The **other** sizes do not fit.

some*   **Some** kids like to swim. **Some** don't.

their*   They clapped **their** hands.

*tested high-frequency words

Pictionary

party

stars

33

Contents

Story Time

Let's Find Out

36 Story Time
Check out a book!

44 The Tale of a Book
Meet two men who make books.

54 A Big Fish Tale
What is fishy in this tale?

62 Make a Book
Tell your own tale!

See page 63 for My New Words and Pictionary!

Story Time

Come in! Come in! We think you will like our place.

This big, big place is filled with books. We like books! Why? We will tell you.

This place has lots of water.

Books can help us see new places.
See this picture? This place has lots
and lots of water!

Deserts

This place is hot and dry.

See this? This place is hot and
dry. You can see any place at all.
A book will take you there.

Books can help us try new things.
Make yummy snacks. Sing silly songs.
Get games to pass on to friends.

What other fun things can we try?
Just grab a book and take a peek.

Will this book bring smiles? Books
can make us feel happy. Books can
make us feel lots of things.

What will *you* get from books?
Just pick them up and see!

The Tale of a Book

by Alice Johnston

Do you like books? Books can
take us places and tell us tales.

But books do not just pop up
in shops. Books are made. Let us
see how.

Andrés Pi Andreu

These men are friends. They work together to make books.

Luis Contreras

This man thinks up tales.

This man makes pictures.
His pictures match the tales
his pal tells.

This man thinks of a tale. Will it be funny? Will it make kids think?

Will he tell a tale of a trunk sunk in deep water? Will he tell of bees that sting and bells that ring? He can! He can tell any tale he thinks up.

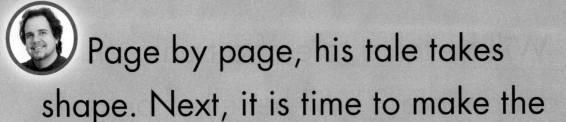 Page by page, his tale takes shape. Next, it is time to make the pictures. But he can not make them.

 His friend can! His friend looks at the tale. It is time for him to think and plan.

51

He plans his pictures. He adds this. He adds that. The pages fill up.

The pals grin. "This will be our new book! We think it tells a funny tale. We hope you will like it!"

A Big Fish Tale

by Anthony King

illustrated by Jeff Ebbeler

Mom and Hank have a big, big book. It has pictures from the past.

Hank grins and winks at Mom.
"Sis, we can tell lots of tales."
"Tell us! Tell us!" my friends and
I beg.

"One time Hank and I went
fishing," Mom tells us. "Hank got a
bite and yanked on his pole."

Mom goes on, "But that fish
yanked back, and Hank fell in! I had
to think fast. Hank could sink!"

"I tossed our new rope out to Hank, and he hung on. But that did not help a lot."

"Just then some ducks passed by.
I tossed that rope up in the sky. And
can you tell what they did next?"
"Tell us! Tell us!" we cry.

Hank tells the rest. "Those ducks lifted me out of the water. But then I had to let go. If I had not, I could still be flying!"

Mom and Hank can not hide big grins. Then we get it.

"That is not just any old tale!" we cry. "That is a big fish tale!"

Make a Book

1 Fold the paper in half.

2 Fold the top side back.

3 Flip the book over. Fold this side back too.

4 Write your story. Add some pictures.

5 Show off your new book!

This is Rex.

Rex likes to dig.

Look what Rex digs up.

Rex rules!

My New Words

any*   Do you have **any** pets?

friend*   I like my **friend.**

new*   This hat is old and not **new.**

our*   **Our** class has fish in a tank.

*tested high-frequency words

Pictionary

book

picture

water

Contents

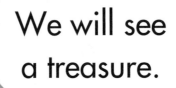

Treasures
in the U.S.A.

Let's Find Out

66 Treasures in the U.S.A.
The U.S.A. has so much to see!

72 A City, A Gift
How can a city be a gift?

78 The Big Surprise
What is the big surprise?

84 Treasure Hunt
Can you figure out these clues?

Treasures in the U.S.A.

Fly with me! The U.S.A. has much to see. Just look at this place! The land rises up, up, up to the sky.

Here is a place with waterfalls. Crash! Splash! Rushing water makes mist. Sunshine on this mist makes a band of colors.

This place in the West has tall, tall trees. Try standing beside one. You will feel as small as an ant!

This is one of five huge lakes. Kids can fish, swim, and dig in the sand. Do you wish you were there?

Did you know that water runs deep inside Earth? We can see it inside caves like this.

Our last stop is these cliffs. Look at their size!

Now our trip is done. I hope you will fly with me again.

A City, A Gift

by Greg Browning

illustrated by Bob Masheris

A city is a place. But did you know that a city can be a gift? A city is a gift when it has lots to see and do.

A city can be next to water. It can be next to big hills. These are good places for a city.

This city is beside water. Lots of
ships pass by here again and again.
Why not take a ride on one?

There is much to do here. Fish at sunrise. Rest on benches when you are done. Then swim. A city next to water is a gift!

This city is next to big hills. There is much to do outside here. Hike on paths. Sniff! Smell fresh grasses.

If you were to look, you could see tracks left by foxes. A city next to big hills is a gift!

The Big Surprise

by Iris Rashid
illustrated by Tammie Lyon

"Here it comes!" yells Shak.
Bus 10 stops and Shak rushes on.
"What will we see on this trip?" he
asks Dad.

Dad flashes a smile. "If I were to
tell, then it will not be a surprise!"
"Can I get a hint?" Shak asks.

1. big
2. green
3. gift

Shak gets his notepad from his backpack.

"We will see something big," Dad tells him. "Its color is green. It came to us as a gift."

Shak thinks and thinks. What on Earth can it be? Then Dad drops a new hint. "See that big ship? It will take us to see her."

Shak looks this way and that.
Then he jumps up. "I see it, Dad!"
he yells. "I see the big gift!"

Dad has passes to get inside. When they are done, he wishes to know what Shak thinks.

"Here is a hint," Shak tells him. "Take me on this trip again!"

Treasure Hunt

Read the clues. Match each clue with a picture.

1. Water falls from me.
2. We grow in a forest.
3. I stand tall. I am green.
4. You can swim in me or play on my beach.
5. I am under the ground.

lake

redwood trees

Statue of Liberty

waterfall

cave

My New Words

again*   Come **again** to play.

colors   Red and blue are **colors**.

done*   She is **done** with her homework.

know*   I **know** where it is.

mist   **Mist** is very small drops of water in the air.

were*   We **were** cold and hungry.

*tested high-frequency words

Pictionary

Earth

Contents

Special Places

88 Let's Find Out
Special Places
These places are fun!

96 Clark at the Zoo
What will Clark see?

104 A Place for Molly
Where can Molly go?

108 Hideaway
Find hidden things!

See page 109 for My New Words and Pictionary!

Special Places

Home is a nice place for us. We smile and hug. We eat and talk.

At home with Gram and Gramps is nice. Time with them is lots of fun.

The shore is a nice place too.
Every June, the four of us have fun.
We swim in the sea and dig in the
sand. Then we swim more!

We hope it does not storm. If it storms, we must get off the shore.

This is a fun place to see a game.
This sport has three bases and a
home plate. Men bat and run.

We clap and yell if they score
a run. We jump up if they hit a ball
to us.

Does this place look fun? We
can see fish of every size and color.
These fish can look back at us!

This porch is a nice place. Mom and I sit and talk on the swing. We like this place best of all!

Clark at the Zoo

by Owen James

illustrated by Kathy Couri

Clark likes to see animals. He can see them all in this one place. It is the zoo!

The zoo is like a big park for animals. Mom, Dad, Clark, and Star go every fall. What will Clark see this time?

Clark sees this big cat sleep. It likes sunny spots. It snores in the sunshine.

Clark sees this white cub jump off the rock. A big ice cube makes the water cold. This cub likes chilly spots.

Mom, Dad, Clark, and Star want snacks. Mom gets popcorn and four drinks. It is fun to rest on this bench.

Next Clark sees this snake. Will it harm him? Not at all! All the animals are safe to see at this place.

It is time to pet barnyard pals.
Clark can pet rabbits, pigs, or sheep.
Which farm animal does Clark
like best?

Did Clark see lots of animals? Yes! He saw them all in this one place. He saw them at the zoo!

A Place for Molly

by Audrey Lin • illustrated by Ilene Richard

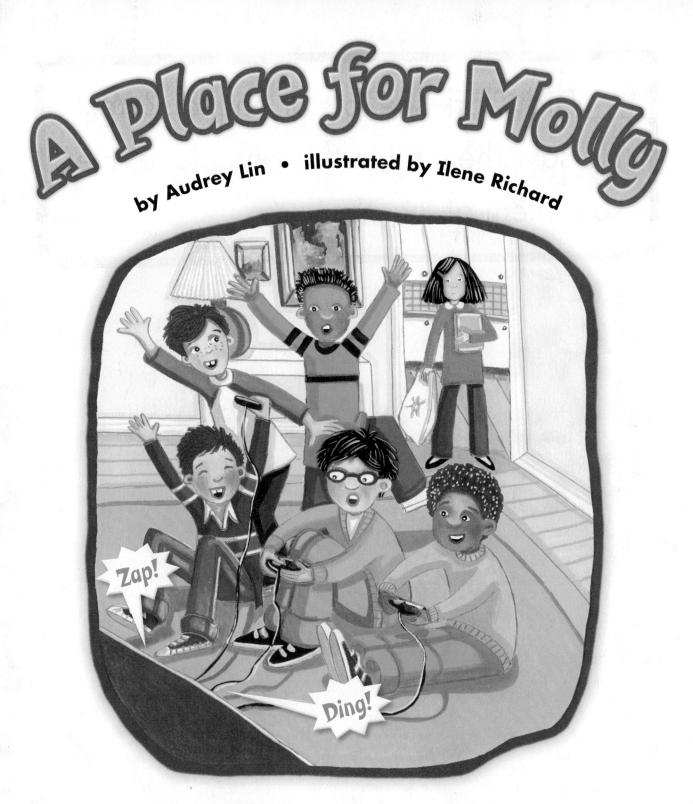

Molly needs a place just for her.
Mark is in here with four pals. This is
not the place for Molly.

Dad fixes the car in this place.

Beep! Beep! He tests the horn.

He makes the car go on and off.

This is not the place for Molly.

Molly checks the yard. *Arf! Arf!*
Her dog Pork Chop barks and barks.
Her cat Dart hisses. It is like a zoo!
This is not the place for Molly.

Does every spot have someone in it? Yes, but look! This place is not for Mark or Dad. It is not for Pork Chop or Dart. This place is just for Molly!

Hideaway

Cory is in his special place. Help him find these hidden things.
corn, fork, horn, jar, yarn

My New Words

cold
This ice is **cold!**

does*
Does she skate well?

every*
Every child needs to bring a book to class.

four*
Four is one more than three.

off*
The cat jumps **off** the bed. The radio is **off.**

*tested high-frequency words

Pictionary

sea

zoo

Contents

Treasures at Home

Let's Find Out

112 **Treasures at Home**
Check in a box! Check in a bag!

118 **Yard Sale**
A yard sale is hard. But it is fun!

128 **Mom's Treasures**
What did Mom have when she was a girl?

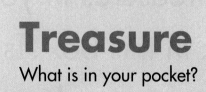

134 **Treasure**
What is in your pocket?

See page 135 for My New Words and Pictionary!

Treasures at Home

Are there treasures in your home? Check in this box. Is there something you forgot about?

Is it a small car? Is it a truck? Is it this fur bunny you once curled up with? This can be a nice treasure.

Check family snapshots. Pick one that makes you smile. Is it you and your family all together?

Is it Mom or Dad? Is it you with pets? Is it your dog or bird? What is his name? What is her name?

Check inside bags. What treasure
will you see first? Is it in a box? Is it
in a jar?

Is it sweet? Is it salty? Is it crunchy?
Is it yummy? Did Mom or Dad get it
for you? All these can be treasures.

Yard Sale

by Emma Trudley ★ illustrated by Mick Reid

We had lots to do for the yard sale.
Running a yard sale is hard! But it is fun.
First we planned the date for the sale.
Then we made an ad.

Next my family picked things to sell. Mom had about fifty things. Tim gave shirts. Sis gave her purse. I gave my stuffed fur dog.

Then we made price tags for things.
How much for this purse? What is the
price for an old fur dog? We spent lots
of time tagging things.

We needed to tell everyone where
to go. We had fun with this job!

We had black and green and
red to do the job. It was messy.
But together we did a good job.

We put things on benches. Then it was about time for the sale to start.

At nine, moms and dads and kids
started to drive up. Cars parked at the
curb. Our time for sitting had passed!

More came. They shopped
and shopped. Mom was the clerk.
I helped. I sat with the cash box.

Once I asked a man, "Did you get a treasure?" He grinned and hugged his bag of stuff.

Running a yard sale is hard! But my family had fun together. We will plan a yard sale again next fall!

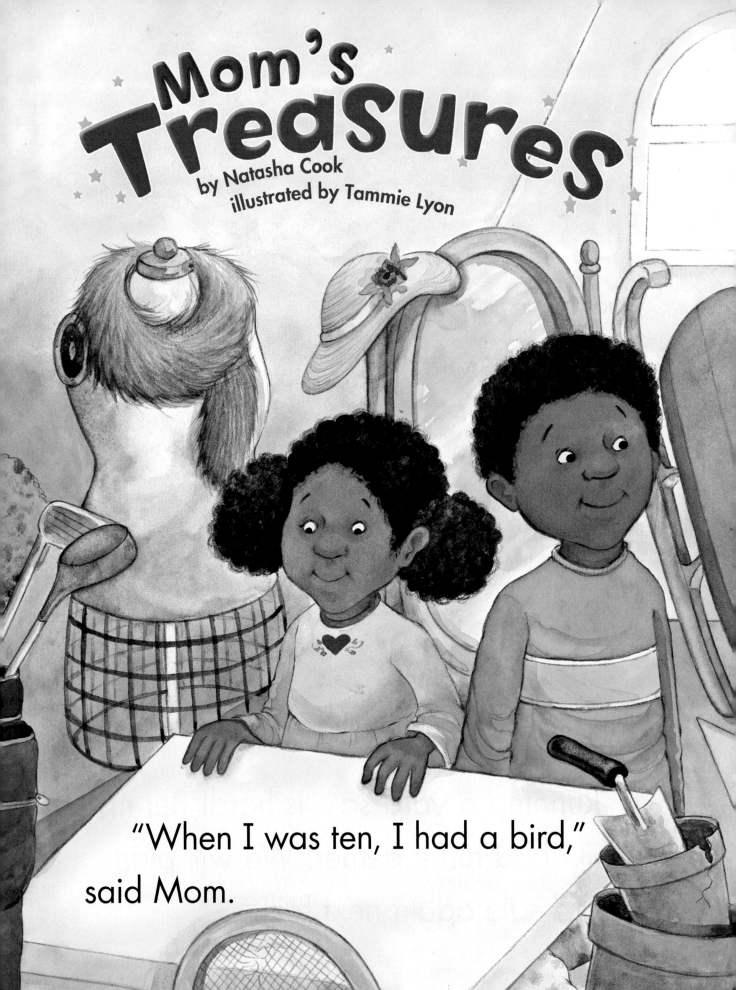

Mom's Treasures

by Natasha Cook

illustrated by Tammie Lyon

"When I was ten, I had a bird,"
said Mom.

"This is her cage. It is very old. I can still see my bird sitting on this perch singing tunes."

"This is my jump rope," said Mom. "It is not that old. All my pals skipped rope together on my sidewalk. I can still see us jumping and grinning."

"My dad once had a tan horse,"
said Mom. "This went on her back.
It is not that old. We trotted on a
path about ten miles."

"This is very old," said Mom. "It is a churn. It turns thick milk into butter. My family has kept it all this time."

"Next week, we will go shopping for milk. Then we will use the churn and make butter together. Old things can be new again!"

Treasure

by Lee Bennett Hopkins

A rusty door key,
A part of a tool,
A dead bee I was saving
to take in to school;

A crust of pizza,
Sand from the shore,
A piece of lead pipe,
An old apple core;

My library card,
A small model rocket—
I guess it is time to clean
out my pocket.

My New Words

about*   This book is **about** trains.
             About 12 cans can fit
             in the box.

family*   The people who take care
             of you are your **family**.

once*   **Once** means one time.
             Once is also a time
             in the past.

together*   Mix the milk and egg
             together.

treasures   **Treasures** are things that
             are very special to you.

*tested high-frequency words

Pictionary

perch

Contents

Sharing with Neighbors

Let's Find Out

138 Sharing with Neighbors

We can all share.

144 Great Gardens

What makes gardens great?

150 Great Helpers

See how help can make a job go fast!

158 Come to the Block Party

This will be lots of fun!

See page 159 for My New Words and Pictionary!

Sharing with Neighbors

People need many things for jobs.
Ann will ask her pal Sammy for help.

Can she use his green rake? He's happy to give this rake to her. She's going to rake her yard now.

Many kids share things. Jim has big trucks and small trucks. He's happy to share.

Jim will let his pal use his trucks.
That's nice of him. This pal will share
his cars with Jim next time.

Many kids can share how to make
things. This girl likes crafts.

She can make cute things. She's telling her pals how to make these things. It's great when people share!

Great Gardens

by Dominic Lewis • illustrated by Lindy Burnett

These people share a garden. They all have homes close by. Let's take a look.

Here's a rose garden. We can see many pink and red roses.

This is Jill. She tends her rose plants.
She's cutting rose stems with buds on
them. They're for Jen and Nan.

Look at this! Here's a great garden.

We can see many mums.

These kids had luck with big mums and small mums. They're happy to give them to people.

You've seen corn in cans. But have you seen corn plants?

Corn is on tall stalks. Peel back the husks. There's corn on the cob.

People pick corn and fix it to eat.
We all like corn on the cob! It's
yummy in the tummy. It's great!

Great Helpers

by Ashanti Jones • illustrated by Bob Masheris

Sam is going to make a swing set.
"I've got lots of work," he said.
"It will take weeks to make a swing
set by myself."

"I'll ask Ben if he has a big saw."
"Yes," said Ben. "I've got two
saws. I can give you a hand. Let's
get started!"

Sam cut. Buzz! Buzz! Buzz!
Ben cut. Buzz! Buzz! Buzz!

"Now we've got to get a drill," said
Sam. "We need a drill to make holes."
"I will ask Jane," said Ben.

"Yes, I've got a drill," said Jane.
"I'll get it, and I can help too."

Sam cut. Buzz! Buzz! Buzz!

Ben cut. Buzz! Buzz! Buzz!

Jane drilled. Hum! Hum! Hum!

Ben and Sam cut. Buzz! Buzz! Buzz!
Jane drilled. Hum! Hum! Hum!
Ben, Sam, and Jane worked hard.

"Thanks, all!" grinned Sam. "Many people helped, and we're done at last. Kids will like this great swing set!"

Come to the

BLOCK PARTY

✸ When: Saturday, July 28, at 2:00 P.M.

✸ Where: Our Block

✸ What to Bring: Food to Share

✸ Games for All . . . . .

Balloon Toss

Egg Toss

Treasure Hunt

Big Bike Parade

Would you like to go to this block party?

My New Words

give*   If you **give** me something, you let me have it.

great*   Something that is **great** is very good or important.

many*   **Many** means a large number or a lot.

people*   **People** are men, women, and children.

*tested high-frequency words

Pictionary

drill

husk

stalk

Acknowledgments

Text

Every effort has been made to locate the copyright owner of material reproduced in this component. Omissions brought to our attention will be corrected in subsequent editions. Grateful acknowledgment is made to the following for copyrighted material.

134 Curtis Brown, Ltd. "Treasure" by Lee Bennett Hopkins first appeared in *Good Rhymes, Good Times: Original Poems* published by HarperCollins. Text copyright © 1985, 1995 by Lee Bennett Hopkins. Used by permission of Curtis Brown, Ltd. All rights reserved.

Illustrations

Cover: Rose Mary Berlin, Kathy Couri, Karen Jones Lee **1, 66–71** Rose Mary Berlin; **3, 86, 96–103** Kathy Couri; **3, 111, 134, 136, 144–149** Lindy Burnett; **4, 22–31** Karen Jones Lee; **5–13** Laura Ovresat; **34–35, 54–61** Jeff Ebbeler; **64, 78–83, 110, 128–133** Tammie Lyon; **65, 72–77, 137, 150–157** Bob Masheris; **87, 108** Remy Simard; **104–107** Ilene Richard; **111, 118–127** Mick Reid; **137–143** Elizabeth Allen.

Photographs

Every effort has been made to secure permission and provide appropriate credit for photographic material. The publisher deeply regrets any omission and pledges to correct errors called to its attention in subsequent editions.

Unless otherwise acknowledged, all photographs are the property of Pearson Education, Inc.

Photo locators denoted as follows: Top (T), Center (C), Bottom (B), Left (L), Right (R), Background (Bkgd)

Cover: (TL) Colin Keates/The Natural History Museum, London/©DK Images, (TL) ©DK Images, (CL) Harry Taylor/©DK Images; **5** (BR) Getty Images; **32** (TR, TL) ©C Squared Studios/Getty Images, (CR, CL, BR) Getty Images, (BL) ©Spike Mafford/Getty Images; **33** (BR) ©Taxi/Getty Images, (BL) Getty Images; **44** (C) ©Dave & Les Jacobs/Getty Images; **62** (C) ©Photos to Go/Photolibrary; **65** (BR) ©Vito Palmisano/Getty Images; **66** (B) ©Robert Glusic/Corbis; **67** (C) ©0169JTB Photo/PhotoLibrary Group, Ltd.; **68** (C) ©Andrew Geiger/Getty Images; **69** (C) ©Vito Palmisano/Getty Images; **70** (C) ©Kenneth Murray/Photo Researchers, Inc.; **71** (C) Jupiter Images; **84** (B) ©0169JTB Photo/PhotoLibrary Group, Ltd., (B) ©Amy Nichole Harris/Shutterstock, (C) ©Andrew Geiger/Getty Images; **85** (BC) NASA; **87** (CR) Getty Images; **88** (C) ©Masterfile Corporation; **89** (C) ©Ariel Skelley/Corbis; **90** (C) ©C Squared Studios/Getty Images, (C) ©Stockdisc/Getty Images; **91** (C) ©David McLain/Aurora/Getty Images; **92** (T) Getty Images, (C) Macduff Everton/Getty Images; **93** (C) ©Yellow Dog Productions/Getty Images; **94** (C) ©Richard T. Nowitz/Corbis; **95** (C) ©Daniel Bosler/Getty Images; **109** (B) ©JTB Photo/PhotoLibrary Group, Inc., (BL) ©Michele Westmorland/Getty Images; **117** (TR) Getty Images; **135** (B) ©Juniors Bildarchiv/Alamy; **159** (BC) Getty Images.